T0065521

LIVING YOUR BEST
Life On Purpose

BISHOP HATTIE DANCIL-SMALL

authorHOUSE®

AuthorHouse™
1663 Liberty Drive
Bloomington, IN 47403
www.authorhouse.com
Phone: 833-262-8899

Published by AuthorHouse 01/27/2021

ISBN: 978-1-6655-1158-2 (sc)
ISBN: 978-1-6655-1159-9 (e)

Library of Congress Control Number: 2020925175

Print information available on the last page.

*Any people depicted in stock imagery provided by Getty Images are models,
and such images are being used for illustrative purposes only.
Certain stock imagery © Getty Images.*

This book is printed on acid-free paper.

CONTENTS

FOREWORD

The Power of Witness

A young Pastor had served for many years in the inner-city.

Many felt that she was wasting her time there. She seemed to have little to show for her efforts, at least in terms of large numbers or an attractive building. But across the years, she had built a good rapport with the street people of the area and had gained their respect. As a result, she could safely go places that others feared to enter.

One night during a meeting at the church, an unshaven, poorly dressed, man entered. This man returned night after night and seemed to listen intently to the sermons. Finally, one night during the invitation, the man came forward. "Do you want to give your life to Jesus?" he was asked by one of the altar workers.

"Well, I don't know", came his reply. "I don't know much about Him."

"Haven't you read in your Bible about Jesus?"

"Nope. I ain't never had a Bible. And besides, I can't read."

"Then, why did you come forward?"

"Well, I'll tell ya, I've been a watchin' that Preacher Lady. She walks like she talks and so whatever she's got, that's what I want!"

Many people will never read the Bible. The only gospel they

will ever know is the one they see written in the lives of Christians. But this kind of message has the power to reach the lives of many people. Bishop Hattie Dancil-Small through the years has and continue to walk out in her lifestyle and witness, the talk she Preach. Knowing her struggle firsthand it is my pleasure to pin this forward.

If the express purpose of this book, Living Your Best Life on Purpose, was to motivate each of you to believe that before you were born God had formed you and shaped you for a particular purpose; mission accomplished! It deals not only in areas of spiritual vulnerability, but gives explicit remedies to overcome, according to the scripture, "with victory."

God wants us to have fellowship with Him and He is always looking for an opportunity to become an essential part of your life "because the Lord's eyes scan the whole world to strengthen those who are committed to him with all their hearts." 2 Chronicles 16:19 CEB

Thank God we are blessed, with this book by such a humble Kingdom servant as Bishop Hattie Dancil-Small, with another tool to bring encouragement, inspiration, and direction to defeat the enemy. In these pages you will find a sound guide to "do justly, love mercy & walk humbly with our God." Micah 6:8

In Living Our Best Life on Purpose, God is sure to see us and be glorified, for He sees us:

As a new creation! "Therefore, if any man be in Christ, he is a new creature: old things are passed away; behold, all things are become new" 2 Corinthians 5:17 (KJV)

As victorious! "Nay, in all these things we are more than conquerors through him that loved us." Romans 8:37

As royalty! "But ye are a chosen generation, a royal priesthood, an holy nation, a peculiar people; that ye should shew forth the praises of him who hath called you out of darkness into his marvelous light;" 1 Peter 2:9

As co-heirs with Christ! "And if children, then heirs; heirs of God, and joint-heirs with Christ; if so be that we suffer with him, that we may be also glorified together." Romans 8:17

As wonderful! "I will praise thee; for I am fearfully and wonderfully made:" Psalm 139:14

With all of this and more plainly outlined for us in this book with uplifting words that speak to our destiny, our purpose, and our future, how can we not Live Our Best Life on Purpose?

Honorable Judge Dr. Janice Y Simmons
Elect Lady of the Sounds of Praise, Kingdom Fellowship Ministries

ACKNOWLEDGEMENTS

God is so good! I give Him all the praise for his direction, protection, and the ability to write my second book, Living Your BEST Life on Purpose! I want to express my deepest thanks and appreciation to Kingdom Harvest Outreach Ministry where I serve as Senior Pastor. I acknowledge your continued encouragement and your faith in me as I serve as your spiritual leader.

To all of you who supported me in purchasing my first book, I am so grateful for your support. I'm thankful to Honorable Judge Jan Y Simmons, the Elect-Lady of the Sounds of Praise for being an example of an awesome Woman of God. I thank you immensely for contributing the forward to this book. Many thanks to the Sounds of Praise Pentecostal Fellowship Ministry, Inc. under the leadership of Chief Apostle Allen H Simmons for your continued support and for always being there for me during the good and not so good times. I'm so glad I said "yes" to serve in ministry.

A special "thank you" to all of my family, my spiritual sons and daughters, and great friends for your continued support. To my only son, George-Kristian, and my grandson, Jahman. I love you more than I have words to articulate. I can't image life without the two of you in it. You can surely testify that I am a living witness of the scripture when it says, "I can do all things in Christ Jesus".

Deacon Donnie Small. The day we said "I do" is one of the most joyous days of my life. Thank you for always being so supportive, loving and kind.

Finally, a special acknowledgement to Sis. Keisha Gunter Blue and **Blue Printz Custom Printables and Designs** for the amazing illustrations. It has been said that a picture is worth a thousand words. Thank you for allowing me to incorporate your custom illustrations into this book. What a blessing you are to the kingdom.

May the Almighty God bless each of you.

DEDICATION

This book is dedicated to some of the most incredibly special and beautiful women of God, I want to thank you for assisting me in making my vision of becoming a successful published author a reality. You are mighty sisters in the Kingdom. Thank you for not being selfish and readily agreeing to help me see my lifelong dream come to pass. Simply saying "thank you" seems so inadequate. But one thing I can do is to continuously pray that whatever you desire in life, and whatever you find your hands to do, it will come to pass. I love you.

Tamika Gibbons, Alice Favors, Angyla Bell and Keisha Blue.
I dedicate this book to each of you.

INTRODUCTION

Live EVERY MOMENT,
Laugh EVERY DAY,
Love BEYOND WORDS.

This is your season to *Live Your BEST Life on Purpose*. For many Christians, it is the belief that our best life does not begin until we meet Jesus after death or the rapture. But it is my belief that God wants us to live our best life now. According to scripture. Jesus said, "I came that you may have life and have it more abundantly". When we live our best life on purpose, it is full of hope, joy, meaning, happiness, and satisfaction. It is not based on the material things and wealth that we have although those things will contribute to living a purpose filled life to the fullest. You are born with natural talents and abilities and living with purpose comes from using these gifts to the fullest potential. To know your purpose in life will take a great deal of soul searching to know who you are and what you are capable of. It also takes great faith to believe we are created with a purpose and calling in life. That's why I have titled this book, "Living your Best Life on Purpose".

The word purpose, according to Webster Dictionary, means the reason for which something is done or created or for which something exists. There are many who question their existence for living, their purpose for life. I submit to you that all you need to do is read the book, not this book, but the BIBLE. Although reading this book will help jumpstart your living your best life. Reading the bible, will provide you with what you need to know regarding God's purpose for creating you. So, let me confirm, that you do have a purpose for living.

A life lesson I have learned is that even doing the worst of times, I still have purpose. No matter how daunting life is, I am still blessed. Problems come and go. That's life. When we can see no way humanly possible for a problem to work out, that's when God steps in. There is a purpose even for the difficult times in your life. Do not see yourself through the eyes of the stressful moments or difficult times but see yourself as God sees you. One way I have come to have less stress in my life is to create stress-free moments. Make time to tune everything and everyone out. Listen to your favorite music, drink your favorite tea, sit in your favorite chair, and meditate on the Lord. Just for a few minutes, maybe five or ten minutes or longer if you can. Upon rising, take in some deep breathes and feel the power of the Holy Spirit provide peace in the midst of the stressful situation. As you travel throughout the day, use your tongue to speak positive words over yourself. Speaking affirmations to yourself on a daily basis is a positive way to improve your self-confidence and the relationship with yourself. Here are a few positive affirmations to speak over yourself on a daily basis:

1. **I deserve to be happy.** - This isn't in reference to money or fame. It's simple happiness, however you perceive it. You

deserve your happiness. You deserve to be at peace and content with yourself and your life.

2. **I am beautiful**. - You are beautiful on the inside and outside. Whether you think you're too heavy or too skinny, not fit enough or too bulky, lacking certain features or have too many flaws, you are beautiful just the way you are.

3. **I have so much potential**. -Do what you love, keep working towards your goals. There are some things only you can do. God made you that way.

4. **I am amazing.** For everything you do, you are amazing. With everything you juggle and deal with on a normal basis, and everything you accomplish, you are amazing. For everything people know about you or don't know, you are amazing. Don't let anyone tell you otherwise.

Today, as you begin to read this book, you will start to soar higher than you ever did before. God says we can soar on wings like an eagle. These are the moments when everything is clicking. No problems, no burdens, no hardships. Everything seems perfect. That's the feeling I want to have all of my life, even in difficult times. That's living your best life on purpose. When you live your life on purpose you will begin to soar higher in your daily walk with the Lord. May this book make the difference you need to "Live Your Best Life on Purpose".

CHAPTER 1

Get Pass Your Past

This too shall pass...

You cannot change your past. My advice to anyone who desires to live their best life is to get pass your past. Living in the past will only cause you to lose focus and become stagnant. Stagnation is the state of not flowing or moving. It is the lack of activity, growth, or development. It is a situation in which something stays the same and does not grow and develop: Today, choose to become forward looking and forward moving. These two scriptures both speak of getting pass your past and reaching forth to a new and bright future in Christ Jesus.

Philippians 3:13-14 - Brethren, I count not myself to have apprehended: but this one thing I do, forgetting those things which are behind, and reaching forth unto those things which are before,

I press toward the mark for the prize of the high calling of God in Christ Jesus (KJV).

Isaiah 43:18-19 - "Do not remember the former things, nor consider the things of old. Behold, I will do a new thing, now it shall spring forth; Shall you not know it? (KJV)

Do you sometimes feel like you are stuck in a rut or have you settled for less of an existence than what you were called by God to live? Have you ever thought, "Is this it, or is this all there is?" Has something kept you in the place of mediocrity? Have you settled, gotten sidetracked or disappointed to the point of paralysis? Perhaps it's time for you to move forward. A quote I found says, "Refuse to be average. Let your heart soar as high as it will." Soaring high like an eagle. In this season, God wants us to soar above all that which gets us down and depressed and upset. The Apostle Paul saw that moving forward was a continual pursuit of all that God had for Him or, "The prize of the upward call of God in Christ Jesus." You cannot live your best life without getting past your past. That means letting go of the past and coming to the realization that God wants to give you a fresh new start! I have found myself having pity parties about the past things of my life. But no one attended the party but me. I found myself all alone which is where the enemy wanted me to be. At those moments, Satan was laughing at me because he had me right where he wanted me to be alone, sad, despondent with my focus taken off of God and the great things he has for me. One day I said no more. I'm moving forward. Life is too short for me to linger and remain in the place of do nothing. And I literally got up and began to move and seek God for direction and purpose for my life.

I have found that we all need to be motivated in some area of our lives. Motivation is a force or influence, the act or process of giving someone a reason for doing something. Within the pages of this book, I hope you will find the motivation you need to set goals and make your dreams come to pass. Providing encouraging words are powerful tools. When someone is discouraged or having a difficult time, the right words can clear their outlook and lift their spirits. Other times, there may be a person who does great work and need to be encouraged and motivated along the way, and then there are others who need a little push to finding their purpose and living life to the fullest. I have found that the right words from someone makes all the difference. I pray that this book will encourage you to live your best life on purpose. Hopefully as you read, you will find the tools and motivation to do just that.

We are not able to read a crystal ball or read into the future but there are some things that you must do to leave the past behind and move forward into the new. Yes, even in this season of perilous and challenging times, let us not look back, because even in darkness, there is light in Jesus Christ. The bible tells us that each new day is the day that the Lord has made, and we are to rejoice and be glad in it. So, whatever did not go well on the yesterdays of your life, start new today and move forward. It is with this attitude that Isaiah tells us that the Lord will do a new thing. (Isaiah 43:18-19 - "Do not remember the former things, nor consider the things of old. Behold, I will do a new thing, now it shall spring forth; Shall you not know it?)

To move forward, we must learn to forgive ourselves for past mistakes and sins. Even though God forgives us, we sometimes find it difficult to forgive ourselves. Often times we may find ourselves looking backward either on the good times or the bad times we may have had. Sometimes we focus on the past and pine away at the things we used to have and may have lost. The relationships we used to be in and didn't work. The promotions we missed out on. The money we wasted. The people that hurt us. We all have a past, but do not allow that past to dictate your future. Each of us know someone who continues to live in the past pains and past hurts of life and find themselves stuck.

The Lord spoke through a preacher friend, who said, "No more will you rehearse the past over and over. No more will you keep revisiting old wounds and past pain. No more will torment and oppression, and overwhelming voices of fear stunt and stall you from moving forward. No more will you live under the weight and power of words cast over you that has caged you. No more will you entertain lies and insecurities that have kept guiding you off your road to your destiny. No more will you be baited and tricked into selling yourself short, settling for less than Gods best and living in the fullness of His intention for your life. No more will you see yourself as anything less than how your Father sees you. I submit to you today that people will be transformed because of who you are in Christ Jesus. No more will you allow the enemy to stop you and taint you and burden you. No longer will allow anything or anyone stop you from being all that God has birth in you. Do not abort what God has planted inside of you because you refuse to move forward. You will give birth in this season and nothing will be able to stop it from coming to pass. No more will you walk weak and wounded but from this day forward you will receive strength and power and step into your rightful place as more than a conqueror, seated in Christ, and living out of the abundance of the Kingdom. You should be saying to yourself, no more.

How do you see yourself? Even on my worst days, I see myself as God sees me. He does not see me based on the house I live in or the car I drive, or the business I own, or the people I know. He sees me as his child. That's why each morning, I proclaim: I am the righteousness of God. I am delivered and set free. I am more than a conqueror. I am victorious. My prayer each morning is that God will break any barrier that is hindering my advancement.

No one wants to be stagnant. Always in the same place. Never improving, never doing better. God does not want us to be backward looking, going through life looking in the rear-view mirror. If we drive looking in the rear-view mirror, we will crash. And there are those who crash. We so often can't help ourselves. We remember the hurts of the past and the mistakes we made. It's time now to look ahead and focus on what's before us. God wants to do a new thing in our lives. He wants us to rise up to our full potential in Him. He has called us to do mighty things. He will even make a way when we feel lost and refresh us when we feel burned out. Let us declare that we must keep moving forward. It's only in moving forward that we can ever accomplish what God has called us to. We can't stay where we're at, nor can we go backwards. The only direction we can go is forward. Yes, it can be hard—but it's the only way if we want to move on in God and grow. Don't be afraid to keep moving on, for what was before, now has gone. Remember God has not given us the spirit of fear, but of power, and of love, and of a sound mind. In this season, God wants to accomplish so much more in our lives. Don't blame the pandemic, or your problems and situations of life, God has not stopped blessing us. He has not stopped promoting us. All we have we have to do, stop looking back and move forward in the Lord.

BRETHREN, I COUNT NOT MYSELF TO HAVE APPREHENDED:
BUT THIS ONE THING I DO,
FORGETTING THOSE THINGS WHICH ARE BEHIND,
AND REACHING FORTH UNTO THOSE THINGS WHICH ARE BEFORE,

PHILIPPIANS 3:13

Here are some ways to Move Forward –

#1 - Claim all your territory. The Lord says to Joshua, in Joshua 1:3 *Every* place that the sole of your foot will tread upon I have given you, as I said to Moses". God is saying to us, "Don't let the enemy take anything from you that He has promised to give to you". We must continuously keep moving forward. Not that we won't have setbacks and go through different seasons in our walk with The Lord, but as we keep persevering, we will never exhaust the wealth of God's goodness that is available. He invites us to come, and then to keep coming, and then to come some more. There is continual revelation and new and wondrous things He wants to show us. Go for it. If there is something that has stopped you, get up and get going. That's where you will find your strength and renewal to keep moving forward.

#3 - **Have a bulldog attitude and let nothing stop you.**

God says to Joshua in chapter 1, verse 5 (KJV): "No man shall be able to stand before you all the days of your life; as I was with Moses, so I will be with you. I will not leave you nor forsake you. Be strong and of good courage". Nothing or nobody can stop the promises of God. Just trust Him. They will come to pass. You are invincible in God's will. You may have become afraid of trying new things. You may have been burned out or let down. You may have a fear of failure. Whatever it is, "Be strong and courageous" because where God commands you to go is where you are destined to go. Patience is good, but never let patience turn into stagnation. When it's time to move, go in the boldness of the Lord. Let nothing stop you.

#3 – Be prepared. Joshua, 1:10 – "Then Joshua commanded the people, saying "Prepare provisions for yourselves, for within three days you will cross over this Jordan, to go in to possess the land which the Lord your God is giving you to possess". Preparation is key. When God moves us forward, He has also prepared us for what's ahead. We will never be led where we haven't been equipped. If God is moving, that means you are ready. Much of what has happened to us is to prepare us. So, don't despise those times that may be unpleasant. Embrace them by faith, knowing that you are being prepared to move forward. Embrace whatever has happened to you in the past, that those times were only steppingstones to what is greater.

#4 – Keep moving - There are not stopping points. When you have made the decision to move forward, there should be no stopping points. There will be plenty of reasons to stop, but none of them are good. The way to go is forward. Don't let anything get in the way. There are no boundaries of what God can do in your life. The sky is the limit, especially with God who wants to do more than you can ever imagine. May this season of your life be a season of a new normal, greater territory, higher heights, and deeper depths. I am reminded of the scripture in 1 Chronicles 4:10 "And Jabez called on the God of Israel saying, "Oh, that You would bless me indeed, and enlarge my territory, that Your hand would be with me, and that You would keep me from evil, that I may not cause pain!" So, God granted him what he requested". The name Jabez means pain and sorrow. Why would his mother give him such a name? Every time his name was called, Jabez was re minded of pain and sorrow. Instead of feeling sorrowful for his himself, he sought the Lord and the Lord answered him and provided all that he requested. Let's look at that prayer again: He prayed, "Oh, that You would bless me indeed, and enlarge my territory, that Your hand would be with me, and that You would keep me from evil, that I may not cause pain! Sometimes the pain that we have endured we inflict on others. He said to the Lord, those that inflicted pain on me, don't let me do same to others.

As you reflect back, you will find yourself shouting, see what the Lord has done. I'm moving forward and living my best life on purpose. In this season let us rejoice, and give God the praise. Our testimony will be "God did it!" Will you declare this with me today, "I'm getting pass my past".

CHAPTER 2

Take a Look in the Mirror!

God always sees the best in you, but oftentimes we do not always see what Gods sees. God sees a lot of value in you; God sent His Son for you and not just for a select few. Although there may be those around you who will act as if they are more exclusive and special to Him than you are, remember in God's eyes you are equally important. God sees glorious things in you, and He knows full well what you are capable of. And so, when God looks at you—He sees what others don't or refuse to see in you. The gospel singer Marvin

Sapp sings a song "He Saw the Best in Me". The lyrics say, "He saw the best in me, when everyone else around me, could only see the worst in me. He's mine and I'm His, it doesn't matter what I did. He only sees me for who I am." So, my friends, take a look in the mirror and see what God sees. 1 Samuel 16:7 says, ". . .man looks at the outward appearance, but the Lord looks at the heart." Those words were written for misfits and outcasts. God uses them all. Moses ran from justice, but God used him. Jonah ran from God, but God used him. Rahab ran a brothel. Sarah ran out of hope, Lot ran with the wrong crowd, but God used them all. And David? Human eyes saw a teenager, smelling like sheep. Yet the Lord said, "Arise, anoint him, for this is the one!" (1 Samuel 16:12). God saw what no one else saw— one seeking the heart of God. All that God wants, or needs is someone after His heart. Others measure you by your waist size or wallet. Not God. He examines heart.

Many people live in bondage to feelings of rejection and don't even realize it. It causes them to believe lies about themselves and project hurtful emotions toward others. It also undermines your relationship with God. I know from experience that rejection hurts. That's because at one time it mattered what others thought about me rather than what God thought about me. I am reminded that Jesus Himself also experienced rejection. But unlike some of us, He didn't question who He was. He didn't defend Himself. He didn't deny the hurt that He experienced. And yes, He did experience personal pain, but He went right on telling everyone about the love of God.

In our western society, we value outward appearances. We spend thousands and thousands of dollars on face lifts, behind lifts, and everything in between. We value our looks which isn't bad because we should want to look our best. We value those first impressions, in a job interview or when meeting someone new. We worry about our weight, our hair style, or our own attempts to exercise and diet. There seems to be that goal of wanting to keep up with the Jones. But oftentimes we do not know what the Jones went through to get where they are.

In the story of David, we know from scripture that he was almost overlooked. His own dad forgot about him. When Jesse lines up his eligible sons to pass in review before Samuel, he forgets about David, out in the fields tending the sheep. Samuel looked at the oldest son and thought, "This fellow looks like a king. It must be him!" But God said no. On and on it went, with the second and the third, and the rest of the sons. Samuel cries out in exasperation, "Is this all you have?" Then Jesse remembers David, out in the fields caring for the sheep. David is fetched and when David walks in, the Lord gives Samuel a thumbs up, and Samuel says, "That's the one!" This story of David is for you. There will be a time when you walk into your open door and God says, you are the one. Don't worry about rejection. Don't fret yourself if you are looked over. Your time will come. I want to share the following points to encourage you. I want you to realize everyone is different and unique and God made you that way. Note the following points if you want to live life on purpose:

Point # 1. Don't let What Others Think Take You off Focus

Yes, you should be concerned about your reputation but when people criticize you falsely; when they lie on you, and disrespect you, this shouldn't be something that dominates your mind. If you're one of those people who constantly worry what others think of you, I would like to help you reverse those unpleasant thoughts.

No matter what it is that you obsess about — stop trying to look good for complete strangers, stop listening to rumors, stop pleasing others instead of yourself. The late Bishop G. E. Patterson once said, "I had to be delivered twice in my life, first I was delivered from sin and then I was delivered from people". The word of God says, "For if God be for you, who can be against you". When we are concerned about the negativity coming from other people, we need to overcome this. I know this because I was once obsessed about what others thought about me until I realized that it is only what God thinks of me that really counts. If I live my life the way God expects me to live, what others think is not that important to me anymore. People who don't obsess about what other people think tend to look at the big picture. You only get one chance at life; are you going to allow other people's thoughts to make it less enjoyable? Are you going to let someone's opinion occupy your mind?

Point # 2: Become More Confident in Yourself

I once heard a preacher say, "What you think about me is none of my business" and I believe that this is a good rule to go by. I cannot control someone else's thoughts, nor do I want to. If you think ugly thoughts about someone else, it is strictly between you and God. We need to have confidence in ourselves not to the point of arrogance—but to the point where we believe that "I can do all things through Christ who strengthens me." I meet many people who have low self-esteem and little, if any, confidence in their own selves. There is a tremendous power that occurs when you combine believing in God and believing in yourselves. People will try to place you in a box, and even expect you to follow their definition of who you are. But you know who you are in Christ Jesus. You are not what others think you are. You are what God knows you are. Concerning yourself with what others think can hurt your confidence. Don't entertain the discouraging thoughts of others.

Point # 3: Become Aware of your Life

It seems everyone wants to tell you about your sins, flaws, and shortcomings. Unless it's coming from a place of genuine concern, it's really no one's business. You know you better than anyone else other than God. The reality of sin in your life is uncomfortable and sometimes even painful to look at or think about. Ask God for forgiveness from a repentant heart and move on. It is important to realize that reflecting is not about feeling guilty and it is certainly not to make you feel depressed or sad even though you may find yourself feeling down when you think about how many times you have missed the mark. It is important to be able to be honest with yourself, and with God, about your entire self. God does not just love you when you are good. Let me repeat myself, God does not just love you when you are good. When I was yet a sinner, He loved me. How do I know because He sent his son Jesus to die for me?

For sure, man will ostracize you, reject you and criticize you even in the house of God, which is totally against the Word of God. The word tells us "Brethren, even if anyone is caught in any trespass, you who are spiritual, restore such a one in a spirit of gentleness; each one looking to yourself, so that you too will not be tempted." –Galatians 6: 1. Notice it doesn't say to totally ignore anyone; treat them as if they were a leper and hope they would just simply go away. When you become aware of your sins, please don't do what so many other people do which is simply go on living a sinful life because they believe that God could not possibly forgive them. Look at David in Psalm 51: 1 - 3 when he sinned with Bathsheba. "Have mercy on me, O God, according to your unfailing love; according to your great compassion blot out my transgressions. Wash away all my iniquity and cleanse me from my sin. For I know my transgressions, and my sin is always before me." David was sorry for his transgressions against God and was indeed forgiven by God. Our sin is why Jesus came to earth in the first place; He came to set the captives (which includes you and I) free.

Take a look in the mirror. You are one of a kind, an original. You are not a knock-off, or a fake. You are not who others say you are; You are who God says you are. You can do what God says you can do; You can be whatever God says you can be. Look around you and count your blessings, through your struggles count your blessings, in happy times count your blessings, in troubled times count your blessings. When you look in the mirror, see what God sees. He only sees the best in you.

Your value doesen't decrease based on someone's inability to see your worth

— CHAPTER 3 —

The Magic of New Beginnings

Every once in a while, we all will find ourselves starting over either in a new relationship, or a move to a new house, or in a new job or new position. Starting over isn't always easy. There are those who have the desire to just begin again. There may be those of you who did not graduate school, be it high school, college, or other higher education pursuits. Looking back, you may say to yourself, if I could just start over. There may be some of you who are in a financial bind. If I could just start over, I would not have bought that new dress, or car, or other things that you may have purchased that you did not need. There may be some of you that got in trouble and maybe went to jail or prison. Looking back, you may say to yourself, if I hadn't followed so and so, I would not have gotten in that trouble. If I had it to do all over again, I would do things differently. There may be husbands and wives, that look at your marriage and the mistakes you have made. You may say to yourself, "It would really be wonderful if I could go back to the wedding day and from that day just start all over again. You look back at the things you would like to have done a different way. There may some of you who have wished that when it came to your job or career, you would have made different decisions, if you had the opportunity to do it all over again, But I want you to know that it is never too late to have a fresh new start.

How is it possible for a person to begin again and have a brand-new start? Many of us, if not all of us, have made mistakes in our lives even as Christians. We may have experienced many setbacks and failures in our lives. Sometimes we allow these mistakes, these setbacks, and failures to enslave us to the point that we never enjoy the full Christian life that God has given us to enjoy. In John 10:10 Jesus said, "I am come that you might have life and have it more abundantly." Then he goes on to tell us that there is an adversary, called the Devil, that seeks to steal, kill, and destroy that life. The Devil will remind us of our past to keep us from enjoying the life that God gave us to live in the future. The Devil, our enemy, does not want you to have a fresh start in life. In fact, he wants you to throw in the towel and to give up. In Isaiah 43:18 "The Lord says, 'Forget about what has happened before. Do not think about the past. Instead, look at the new things I'm going to do." Listen to what God is saying in this verse. Forget about what's happened before.

He says don't think about the past. It's over. The book is closed on it. It's time to move on to the next chapter in your life. So, no matter what may be going on in your life, don't give up on God. He is able to do exceedingly, abundantly above all that you ask or think. I have read the end of the book, and it says, you win.

YOU WIN!

If you give up at every negative thing in your life, at every mistake, at every sin, at every problem or situation, you will never arrive at your destination. Press play, fast forward to your future and keep moving. Because your future looks better than you can imagine. We need to understand that God is far more interested in our future than He is in our past. He says, "Forget about your past. Forget about the former things. Don't think about it. Look at the new thing I'm going to do." Speak over yourself: "God is about to do a new thing in me".

Isaiah, the prophet tells us that Israel was being punished for their sins and rebellion against God. Even though they were being punished, God wanted to give hope and encouragement to His people. He wanted them to know that even though they were being punished they were not being forsaken. God wanted His people to understand what they were experiencing would not be the end of them. And that is what God wants you to know that whatever you are going through, it will not be the end of you. The fact is that God wanted to give them a fresh start in life, a new beginning in life. The enemy wants you to think that it is over for you. It's not going to get any better. But that's not God's way. He does not want us to quit. Maybe that is where you are, on the verge of quitting. You feel and believe that you have no future. I once saw on a bumper sticker on the back of a vehicle that "quitters never win, and winners never quit". This is a true statement. Don't quit, it's not over you. God is saying, I have plans for your life. I am about to do something new for you." A new beginning, a fresh start what is being offered to you. Are you ready for the new thing God wants to do in your life? If so, you will begin to live your best life on purpose.

Today you are starting over. This is how you will S.T.A.R.T. Regardless of what kind of setbacks you had in the past. They may have been in your Finances, Relationships, Marriage, or Career. You may have had a moral failure. You may have made some really bad decisions. Maybe you have sinned. Regardless of what may happen in your life, here's how you start over.

S - Stop making excuses. If you want a fresh start in life, you must stop making excuses. You have got to stop seeing yourself as the victim. You have got to take charge of your life. Take charge over your circumstances. Other people can hurt us, other people can harm us, and other people can scar us, but the only person that can ruin your life is you. You have a choice, on how you choose to respond to those hurts. The Bible says that the starting point is to just be honest and accept responsibility for your part in the problem. Proverbs 28:13 "A man who refuses to admit his mistakes can never be successful. But if he confesses and forsakes them, he gets another chance."

T - Take an Inventory of Your Life. You need to take an inventory of your life. That means you need to evaluate all your past experiences. Take an inventory of your life's experiences and learn from them. Galatians 3:4 "You have experienced many things. Were all those experiences wasted? I hope not." The Living Bible says, "Learn from your mistakes. They can be your friend or your foe depending on the way you react to it. You can choose to learn from it or choose to repeat it. Have you said to yourself, this won't happen to me again? I won't do this again. And then you go right back to do the same things. That means you did use those life experiences to learn from them to move forward in life. Instead, you are stuck, and, in some cases, you are going backward. Let me put you on notice, I am never going back. I don't care how terrible things get. Going backward is not for me. Never going back to the how it was.

A - Act in faith. You must launch out into new territory. The Bible says that the key to changing anything is faith. If you want to change your circumstance, it takes faith. If you want to change your personality, it takes faith. If you want to change anything in your life, you must have faith. It takes Faith to go back to school. It takes faith to launch that new business. It takes faith to start over in marriage. It takes faith. Jesus says this in Matthew 9. "According to your faith it will be done to you." That means we tend to get out of life what we expect. "According to your faith it will be done to you." What are you expecting in life? Are things going to be better or worse? Are they going to be the same? If you act in faith, then you will do something positive to ensure that you don't repeat the same mistakes over. The faith I am talking about is an affirmative faith that takes positive action coupled with the help of God to make changes in life. Anybody who know me should know that I am a faith walker. I walk by faith and not by sight. When things seem to go against me, and they do; I just lift my eyes to hills from which comes my help, knowing that my help comes from the Lord.

R - Refocus. You need to refocus your thoughts if you want to change your life. If you want to get going again, if you want a fresh start, you need to rethink the way that you think. You need to change your mind set. Refocus. Take you mind off your mistakes and your problems or the situations that has arose in your life and think about how you can change them. Proverbs 4:23 "Be careful how you think. Your life is shaped by your thoughts." The way you think, determines the way you feel. And the way you feel determines the way you act. If you want to change your actions, just change the way you think, and it will inevitably change the way you act. If you are depressed, discouraged, and distressed it may be because you're thinking depressed, discouraged and distressing thoughts. That's your choice. You don't have to think those thoughts. If you're acting in fearful, worried ways it's because you're thinking fearful, worried thoughts. Romans 12:2 "Be transformed by the renewing of your mind." You must refocus your thoughts to start over, that means you must change your thoughts. Which memories are you still rehearsing that keep you from having a fresh start in life? The Bible says let go. Let go of those things. You must change your mind and let go and get rid of those painful, hurtful memories.

T – Trust. Trust God to help you succeed. Depend on Him. We don't to need depend on ourselves. We've already proven that we can't do it on our own. Some people just don't get it. They stumble and fall and then they get up and say, "I'll just try harder!" It's like you go up to a wall and bang your head against it and the wall doesn't fall. You try it again and Bang! Again. You keep doing it thinking, "Maybe it will fall over this time." That's the definition of insanity – doing the same thing over and over and over and expecting different results. If we keep doing the same thing then we will keep getting the same result. We can't change who we are, only God can do that. I am not speaking about the outward man but the inner man. The real person is the hidden person of the heart. Success in this Christian life is not trying harder but living smarter. It means giving God control of your life. Zechariah 4:6 "You will not succeed by your own strength or power but by My Spirit, says the Lord."

When you give your life to the Lord, you become a brand-new person inside. You are not the same anymore. Old things are passed away, behold all things become new. A new life has begun!" God specializes in new beginnings. Jesus Christ has the power to do that. It's called being born again, the chance to start over. I came to tell you know that you can have a fresh start. It begins now. Are you ready to START?

CHAPTER 4

Just Do You!

Before you can know your purpose, you must know who you are. You must know that there is no one else on the face of this earth who is like you. No one else has your specific DNA. You are one of a kind. David says in Psalms 139:14 (NIV) I" praise you because I am fearfully and wonderfully made; your works are wonderful; I know that full well". This means that you are so amazingly made that you should never doubt who you are. Set high expectations for yourselves.

Oftentimes we expect more of others than we do of ourselves. Try instead to treat yourself the same way you would treat a close friend. Don't say anything about yourself (out loud to others, or even just in your head) that you wouldn't say about someone you care about. Never speak negatively about yourself. You are what you speak. In fact, give negative thoughts and negative people an eviction notice. It can be hard enough for you to believe in yourself, especially if you have developed doubts about your self-worth. No outside influences are needed. If you are having trouble seeing all the amazing things you possess and all the beautiful things you could offer to make this world a better place, change the lens of your eyes and begin to see more clearly. You can take stock of all the things you have already accomplished and set goals for the future. Get a fresh perspective on things, look for opportunities to use your skills, and take good care of yourself to help rebuild your confidence. Believe in yourself. You are braver than you think, more talented than you know, and capable of. Believe in your infinite potential. Your only limitations are those you set upon yourself.

I know sometimes you feel like giving up on your goals and aspirations because failure is a possibility, but it's perfectly natural to struggle with something. Instead of blaming yourself for doing something wrong, stop worrying about the consequences. You must learn to forgive yourself. Make peace and move forward. Forgiving yourself requires empathy, compassion, kindness, and understanding. Forgiveness is important to the healing process since it allows you to let go of the anger, guilt, shame, sadness, or any other feeling you may be experiencing, and move on.

Know your self-worth. Your self-worth is a function of how you value yourself. To build your self-worth you must first discover your values and then make up your own definition of success. I am a believer of speaking to myself and encouraging myself. You must build you up. Work on thinking positively about yourself and your behavior. Fight the urge to be negative by identifying two of your strengths every day. Make sure that you challenge any unproductive thought that enters your head. If you catch yourself thinking negative thoughts like "I am a loser," "no one likes me," and "I can't do anything right," stop yourself and challenge the thought. Counter it with productive thoughts, identifying positive things about yourself. The more that you practice this positive thinking, the easier it will become.

Find ways to keep moving forward. Many of you dwell too much on the past. Paul says in Philippians 3:13-16 (KJV): "Brethren, I count not myself to have apprehended: but this one thing I do, forgetting those things which are behind, and reaching forth unto those things which are before, I press toward the mark for the prize of the high calling of God in Christ Jesus". Dwelling on the past can make you lose sight of your present life. This can make your life quickly pass you by without enjoyment of the present. God has a great future planned for you.

Focusing on who to blame for past hurts can spoil the present. Instead of dwelling on who has caused you pain, forgive them. Focus on present events and leave behind any blame or hurt you feel. If there is someone in your past that has hurt you, choose to forgive and forget. Festering in the pain doesn't harm the person who hurt you and it will cause you to stay in the past. Remember the model prayer that Jesus taught the disciples, "forgive us our trespasses, as we forgive those who trespass against us. Choose to forgive, and then you will be able to live in the present and press into your future. Become the best version of you. Be all that God has ordained you to be. Go forward. Greater awaits you!

------ CHAPTER 5 ------

God will Exceed Your Expectations

It's awesome to know that we serve, an all-powerful, all-knowing, ever present God. He is without limitations. We can depend on him always. There really is nothing too hard for our God. Allow God to exceed your expectations. When we have doubt, God is always faithful. During my years of serving as a Senior Pastor, God has always been faithful. He has proven his faithfulness to me each and every day of these 16 years. God is not confined. You cannot put Him into a box. Your imagination cannot hold him. God will not and cannot be defined and limited to our boundaries, our limits, and our parameters.

God is bigger and greater than anything we can image. The greatest news to me is not that Paul knows Christ, or that John knows Christ, or that Peter knows Christ, but that we, you, and I know Him. The one who is able to do exceeding, abundantly above all that we ask or think. God will blow you mind if you let him! He will exceed your expectations. Whatever your dreams and aspirations are for ministry or for your personal life, God's about to do one better. God wants to top whatever you think or do. Things that you thought were impossible become possible with God. And we will see manifestations (an indication of the existence, reality, or presence of something) and miracles. In our very midst we are about to witness God move in ways we though were improbable if not possible.

Let me encourage you to speak only what God speaks. All things are possible. There are no impossibilities with God. When we say: "It can't happen, or it won't happen, this is too good to be true, already we are counting God out. That's what the naysayers say. That's what the enemy tells us. But God, tells us differently and I choose to believe him. He tells us that we are already victorious. He tells us that we are more than conquerors. He tells us that whatsoever we ask of the father in the name of Jesus, it shall be given to us. God is not passive or indifferent about our lives. If we as believers allow Christ to dwell in us in fellowship, then God will do things "exceedingly abundantly" beyond what we anticipate. The roadblock that hinders you from receiving the manifestations of God is being removed, and if you allow him, he will move them now. Through your relationship with Jesus Christ all that seems impossible now becomes possible. Those changes you want to make in your life, now are possible; That situation that needs to be changed, now is possible; That new career is now possible with Jesus. That disease that the doctors have given up on, healings and miracles are now possible. Financial increase is now possible. Today I entreat you to bind every roadblock, every hinderance, everything that want to stop you will be moved. And not later, but Now.

Prayer is the key that unlocks the spiritual doors of walking in spiritual power. Where the focus is not on the situation, but on God. · You cannot help but win, when we turn our faces, our lives, our whole beings toward Jesus Christ. He overwhelms us! When we put our total trust in him, no matter what it looks like. No matter what it feels like, we are to look to Jesus, the author and finisher of our faith. God is not able just sometimes; He is able all the times. You can always depend on the Lord. He's always there, to help in time of need.

I want to encourage you to pray in faith, asking God to do far beyond all that we can ask or think. Paul tells us in 2 Corinthians 9:8 And God is able to bless you abundantly, so that in all things at all times, having all that you need, you will abound in every good work. Praise the Lord. Thank you, Jesus. God is speaking to you. As situations and circumstances arise, I want you to remember the words God will exceed your expectations. You will see the manifestations and miracles that God has promised. There are no limits in God.

- Allow them to be manifested.
- Expect them. Stand on the promises of God
- See through the eyes of faith.
- Receive them/Embrace them as though you already have them.

CHAPTER 6

Living Your Life on Purpose

God has a purpose for everyone. Every plan you have for your life should begin and end with God in mind first. Purpose is the reason for which something is done or created or for which something exists. PURPOSE as defined by Merriam-Webster's Dictionary is "an anticipated outcome that is intended or that guides your planned actions". Every day you should life your life on purpose.

Sometimes we can be so busy about our lives that we forget the purpose behind them. We are driven by the demands of life and not realizing that God always has a greater purpose. His purposes not only encompass our lives, but the lives of those around us—in our homes, on our jobs, and in our community. In other words, GOD deliberately made each of us with a conscious aim and plan. We are to consider that God has a purpose in each of us to be fulfilled, for we are purposed and perfected with a purpose. We may not have had the best life growing up or even as adults. Apostle Paul encourages us when he says in Romans 8:28 "And we know that in all things God works for the good of those who love him, who have been called according to his purpose". So, it is God who gives us purpose. That's why I don't consult man regarding what

I should do, where I should go, or what I should say. I take it to God. He knows me and He knows my future. He is omnipresent; He is omniscient, He is omnipotent. He is everywhere. He knows everything. And He is all powerful. So why not submit yourselves to Him. While we are trying to figure it out, God in his infinite ways has already worked it out.

These days there are so many what I call pop-psychologists hawking their self-help seminars. Gurus of every kind flood the internet selling their secret formulas and magic portions for a more successful and fulfilling life. We have the psychics who so many will turn to who state they can read your future. Everybody wants to know their purpose. So, we go through life aimlessly looking for it. Everybody knows when they were born. We have a birth certificate to prove it. But very few know why they were born, so they are searching for meaning. Your alarm clock can tell you what time to wake up in the morning, but it cannot tell you 'why' to wake up in the morning.

If I were to ask, how many people believe that God has a purpose for their lives, almost everyone would say yes. Yet if I ask how many know their God-given purpose, I believe few hands would remain in the air. Most people yearn to live meaningful lives. I believe that one of Satan's most powerful lies is to tell you that God does not or no longer has a purpose for your life, or that you will never know your true purpose and that you are here by chance. Satan is a liar. Why do we listen to him? He tells you that your existence is random. He tells you that your life will never get any better. That's a lie and the truth is not in him. Words of encouragement: Seek God. Talk to him. Ask for direction. Stay in his word. David says, "Your word is a lamp to my feet and a light to my path." The Word of God is best shown by the way we live it, by the way that we pay heed to it, by the way that we live it out, and by the way we walk it out.

You see, the truth is that until I found my God-given purpose, my life was driven by self-preservation and self-promotion. In other words, I became my agenda. Keep doing things your way, no matter how good the intentions are, you will not live a fulfilled life. But when you discover God's purpose for your life, you will find something that is greater than you and for what you are willing to give, spend and live your life. Then, instead of living a life of frustration you now are released to live a life of fulfillment.

Many of us give up all too easy and quickly when things don't go the way we want them to go and the way we want them to. We are easily moved and shaken so much so that we never achieve our purpose or our destiny. But the bible tells us to be steadfast and unmovable. If you only knew the value of being connected to God, you would never ever want to be disconnected from Him. So many people stop and give up before realizing their dreams and aspirations. I know that problems arise, situations and circumstances beyond your control happen. But let it be known that you can pursue your purpose in life without being shaken by the trials and tribulations of your life.

In order to reach your destiny, it requires that we let go of the past. Since destiny has to do with the future let go of yesterday. Some of us are living in yesterday, not last week, or last month or last year even, but yesterday. Too many of us live in the past. We still bring up past hurts and past disappointments and setbacks. But your past has nothing to do with where God wants to take you. Paul say in <u>Philippians 3:13-14</u> (KJV), "Brethren, I count not myself to have apprehended: but this one thing I do, forgetting those things which are behind, and reaching forth unto those things which are before, I press toward the mark for the prize of the high calling of God in Christ Jesus". Two more words for you to remember is to simply "Trust God". The first two words were to Seek God. The second two words is "Trust God". Proverbs 3:5-6 - Trust in the LORD with all thine heart; and lean not unto thine own understanding. In all thy ways acknowledge him, and he shall direct thy paths.

Moses sent out spies to the promise land. Their purpose was to bring back a report. Their destiny was to claim the land. They almost aborted their destiny because of the report they brought back. After forty days the spies returned. They were unanimous in reporting that the land was rich and productive. Beyond that, the spies disagreed. Ten of them reported that the people of Canaan were huge giants who lived in fortified cities. These spies concluded that the Israelites were not able to overcome them. There are giants in the land. We look like grasshoppers in our own eyes. Get rid of the grasshopper mentality. A grasshopper mentality is the death of dreams and goals and prevents people from achieving their dreams and plans for the future. But Caleb and Joshua had a different spirit and believed God. They said "Let us enter Canaan land. We are well able to overcome it. The Lord is with us. Do not fear the people of the land." We all need a Caleb and Joshua in our lives. Get rid of the naysayers. Those who will never support you no matter what you do. Your purpose can be found in what you are confessing. Start confessing, I am well able.

There are those who go through life aimlessly not knowing what they are to do with their lives. I want you to know that you are alive on this earth at this moment for a purpose and for a reason. The enemy doesn't want you to operate in your purpose or reach your destiny so when you were a little girl or little boy, he was already setting up distractions or traps that would deter you. He would put people in your life who would say, you will never be nothing or you will never obtain anything in life. But no matter what your situation was or is in life you still have purpose. Why because God gives you purpose. In fact, you were born with purpose. I see that so clearly now. There's a part of me that wants to sit back on my accomplishments and say, "I am done". But God says there is more. Your future looks even brighter. There is greater coming your way.

As you continue to read this book, be encouraged regardless of the situation in your life. You may be low on finances. You may be a single parent. You may have no formal education. Whatever situation you may find yourself in, use it. Use that situation and encourage yourself in the Lord to reach your God given purpose and live life to the fullest. No matter what stage of life you are in, no matter your age, no matter what hindrances lay in front of you, no matter how much you lack in gifts, abilities, or knowledge, God desires to use you in extraordinary ways to expand His kingdom. I believe that I was born to make a difference. That I am not here just aimlessly living my life with no direction and no purpose. Remember, you can do all things, through Christ Jesus who strengths you. It is God who will give you the strength to do what He has ordained you to do. Your purpose is not based on other people but on God. He will use people to propel you to your purpose, but ultimately it comes from God. If God be for you, who can be against you?

Paul tells you that you could be victorious in every situation in your life. Paul overcame all kinds of adversity. In 2 Corinthians 11:23-28 (KJV), Paul says he overcame imprisonments, beaten and whipped; 3 times shipwrecked, in danger of death countless times, in hunger, thirst, cold and exposed but Paul achieved his mission in life. He overcame adversity, hardships, fear, and weakness and achieved his purpose which led to his destiny. We must allow God to be God. He alone is able to help us overcome every situation in which we find ourselves. He uses them to mature us, to change us, to test us and then to position us.

Why is it so hard to find our life's purpose? There certainly is no short supply of problems in this world that need solving. There is no limit on the number of people whom we could help, or inspire, or support. There is no cap on the number of passions we could pursue. Yet, our life purpose often feels hard to pursue. How do you know your purpose? First and foremost, seek God. Sometimes, you may be just exhausted from life and don't know where you will find the energy to fight for what really matters to you. But finding and living your purpose is key to having a meaningful, fulfilling life. That's why I encourage you to spend time with God. He will direct you. Isaiah 40:28-31 (KJV) – says: Hast thou not known? Hast thou not heard that the everlasting God, the LORD, the Creator of the ends of the earth, fainteth not, neither is weary? There is no searching of his understanding. He giveth power to the faint; and to them that have no might he increaseth strength. Even the young shall faint and be weary, and the young men shall utterly fall: But they that wait upon the LORD shall renew their strength; they shall mount up with wings as eagles; they shall run, and not be weary; and they shall walk, and not faint.

Commit yourself unto the Lord. Give yourself wholly unto him. Don't hold anything back. GIVE HIM YOU! The lyrics to an old long by Dorothy Norwood say: "Have your way Lord. Have your way, have your way Lord, Have your way. Do what you want to do. As long as you want to. Have your way Lord. We're here right now have your way". God is looking for those who will say to him, Have your way in my life. Do what you want in my life. I surrender my life to you. God has plans for your life. He says so in Jeremiah 29:11 - For I know the thoughts that I think toward you, saith the LORD, thoughts of peace, and not of evil, to give you an expected end" The Message Bible reads, "I know what I'm doing. I have it all planned out—plans to take care of you, not abandon you, plans to give you the future you hope for". Today you will begin to live your life on purpose.

Live life to
THE FULLEST,
difference make a
along the way

37

CHAPTER 7

From Purpose to Destiny

Destiny is what lies ahead for you. If you don't know your true purpose, then you are apt to be sidetracked, disillusioned, disappointed, and feel hopeless, frustrated, and angry; all of which will hinder you from reaching your destiny. Purpose has to do with the meaning of life. It is about self-worth. Destiny relates to hope, confidence, and assurance. God wants his people to know that He has great plans for their life. When Jeremiah was a little boy, he knew what he was destined to become: Jeremiah 1:4-5 tells us, "Then the word of the LORD came unto me (Jeremiah), saying, Before I formed thee in the belly, I knew thee; and before thou camest forth out of the womb I sanctified thee, and I ordained thee a prophet unto the nations." God already has a purpose for your life even before you were born and what you were destined to become. Destiny according to Webster, are the events that will happen to a particular person or thing in the future. Your purpose propels you into your destiny.

A person's destiny is everything that happens to them during their life, including what will happen in the future. If we are living our lives according to God's purpose, we become masters of our own destiny. Tony Evans says, "Destiny is your customized life calling for which God has equipped and ordained you in order to bring Him the greatest glory and the maximum expansion of His kingdom. When you know what you're here for, there may be a lot of voices, but they don't distract you from completing your assignment here on earth. At the heart of destiny is serving the purposes of God." Never underestimate the value of your life. From the very beginning, God has planned an incredible future for you!

It seems like we are always in a war and for the most part that war is within our minds – it's also in our thoughts and what we set our minds on becomes our reality – our minds dictate how we respond to life, situations, and people. We need to have a renewed mind to win the war against the enemy of our spirit, soul and body and have a mind like Jesus. Stop trying to be like everyone else. Stop trying to be like Mike. Your destiny is not based on what someone else does. Romans 12:2 (NIV) says, "Do not conform to the pattern of this world but be transformed by the renewing of your mind. Then you will be able to test and approve what God's will is—his good, pleasing and perfect will". The word transform means to make a thorough or dramatic change in one's actions, ways and responses to situations and circumstances in and around us. In order words, changed attitudes. The biblical definition of transformation means "change or renewal from a life that no longer conforms to the ways of the world to one that pleases God". This is accomplished by the renewing of your minds, an inward spiritual transformation that will manifest itself in outward actions.

Stop worrying about the past. In Joel 2:25-27 (KJV) we are told "I (the Lord) will repay you for the years the locusts have eaten- the great locust and the young locust, the other locusts and the locust swarm- my great army that I sent among you. You will have plenty to eat, until you are full, and you will praise the name of the LORD your God, who has worked wonders for you; never again will my people be shamed. Then you will know that I am in Israel, that I am the LORD your God, and that there is no other; never again will my people be shamed". As soon as I read this passage of scripture, I knew that God had a word for you. The Lord says, I will repay you. That means everything that the devil stole from you, He will return it. And no man will be able to get the credit for what He is about to do. God will move in such a mighty way, that you will have to say, Only God can do it!

In order to reach your destiny, you must have perseverance, steadfastness, faithfulness, and patience. There is a destiny inside of you that you don't even know about, that you were elected for long before you were born. Suddenly, the Spirit breathes on you and immediately that destiny inside of you is released, it's unlocked, and you become more aware of it. Seek God and his purpose for your life. Only He can confirm what you were elected to do even before you were born? You are the only one who can stop your destiny.

When Samuel had prophesied and laid his hands upon David and said, "You are the King of Israel," did David become the king immediately? No, not according to the Scriptures—it tells us that it took years until David was finally crowned as the King of Judah, and then later the King of Israel. It is important for you to realize— David lived according to his destiny while he was serving his purpose. Destiny is what you are ultimately called to perform in your life. Your purpose is what you are called to perform while progressing to your destiny. What are you called to do right now? David was called to be an armor bearer and psalmist-musician for King Saul; that was his temporary purpose. Later he was a warrior, and then King. Your purpose is always changing and is ever evolving. Your destiny is a very personal path, and no one can walk it for you or tell you where to go. No one can tell you how to change your life in order to live out your meaning of destiny. You must discover your true calling and purpose and allow God to lead you to the life you were destined for.

——— CHAPTER 8 ———

Soaring Higher

God seems to like eagles. They are great symbolic birds of the air. Research shows that there are thirty-three Bible verses that mention eagles! One such scripture is found in Isaiah 40:31: "But those who trust in the LORD will find new strength. They will soar high on wings like eagles. They will run and not grow weary. They will walk and not faint." First and foremost, when God says that we can soar on wings like an eagle, He wants us to soar spiritually in our daily walk with Him. One of the things we know about an eagle is, that they are always up in the air or sitting somewhere on the top of a tree or on the mountaintop. We will never have to stop our car for an eagle, because it wants to cross the road. Eagles are born to fly; they force themselves to soar to great heights and glide on currents of wind; this is placed within them by their Creator. If you ever experience seeing an eagle in flight, it is a sight to behold. We too can soar like an eagle.

The prophet Isaiah uses wings like eagles attributing to the great characteristics of eagles to those who remain faithful to God and look forward to their heavenly reward. The phrase "mount-up" is a translation of the Hebrew word *"alah"*, which means "to go up, ascend, to go up over a boundary." Isaiah is communicating the promise that God will provide renewed strength and courage to overcome obstacles if Israel would only have patience and trust in the Lord's sovereign timing.

You can apply the principle of Isaiah 40:31 by trusting in God's sovereignty and waiting faithfully for Him. "Do not lose heart. Though outwardly we are wasting away, yet inwardly we are being renewed day by day" (2 Corinthians 4:16 KJV)). God in His grace will provide power, strength, and courage to the weary, weak, and downtrodden when they are willing to be patient and wait on Him. God will cause us to mount up on eagles' wings. Eagles' wings are connected with strength.

Even during difficult times, we can soar like an eagle. When navigating through some of life's darkest moments, we must hold unto our faith in God. Our faith is what sustains us, what gets us through challenging times when we, ourselves, cannot see the light at the end of the tunnel. It is in those times that through our faith we trust that God must have a plan, that there must be a greater purpose to our suffering. Without that belief, without that faith, we would have nothing to hold onto, nothing to get us through the dark nights. Faith and trusting in God means believing in God's divine timing and believing that God has the interest of our greater good at heart, even when we cannot see it in the moment. During these difficult and challenging times, this is when you will soar the highest.

What is stopping you from soaring? Now is the time to take

inventory of whatever is holding you back from being your best you. Throw off everything that hinders you and is holding you back. Are you willing to lay it aside? God wants you to soar, but you won't be able to if you're holding on to things or people that is dead weight! If you want to soar in life, you must first love yourself. "You have to love yourself because no amount of love from others is sufficient.

Just as God has placed in every eaglet the desire to fly, He's placed in every believer a vision or dream. A dream that is tightly connected to God's high calling for your life. A desire to reach toward the lofty things He's called you to do. So, when will you stop tolerating your unfulfilled life and start to discover the life you were born to live? Far too few people ever take flight in those dreams because they're afraid to leave the nest. They're afraid to risk rejection. Afraid to fail.

To soar higher mean to think outside of the box, which is a metaphor that means to think differently, unconventionally, or from a new perspective. This phrase often refers to new or creative thinking. I want to warn you that thinking outside the box will feel uncomfortable. You will want to resist this idea, and you will want to go back into the box. So, get ready, God is going to use you as you start to think outside the box.

CHAPTER 9

You are Chosen

God created you for a divine appointment. God has chosen you to make a difference, a unique role only you can fulfil in your life. There is something you can do for God that no one else can do - a God-given niche only you can fill. A chosen person is one who is the object of choice or of divine favor: an elect person. That's who you are. Just think that before God began to create the earth, He was thinking of you. Everything He did, He did it with you in mind. Chosen: Selected, Preferred, Special. Deuteronomy 7:6 says, "For thou art an holy people unto the Lord thy God: The Lord thy God hath chosen thee to be a special people unto himself, above all people that are upon the face of the earth." Originally this was talking about the Children of Israel; but Thanks be to God we too have been grafted in among them and are partakers of the promises of God.

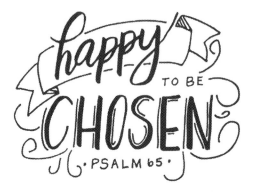

What does it mean to be chosen? To be chosen is to accept the invitation and to do what is necessary to accept the invitation: to give up everything in this world. That is, to say "Yes!" to the calling and then to follow it up with a faithful disciple life. God calls us, but those who are chosen are those who wholeheartedly accept the invitation and its conditions. You are Chosen by God Himself: Jeremiah 1:5 says "Before I formed thee in the belly, I knew thee; and before thou camest forth out of the womb I sanctified thee, and I ordained thee a prophet unto the nations.

Why are there so few who are chosen? Because not many want to pay the price! Jesus says that the gate is narrow, and the way is hard that leads to life, therefore few choose this way. (Matthew 7:13-14) The reason it is hard is that we have to give up everything in this world. Our egotism, our own ideas, opinions, thoughts and feelings, our own will, our own desires. We do this in order to be completely obedient to the leading of the Lord. In order to be chosen, you have to show that you really *want* this life with all of your heart. You can't hold a little back for the world, for relationships, for your self-seeking, etc. It's 100% obedience to Jesus; 100% faithfulness.

No qualifications are necessary. It doesn't matter what our starting point is, who we are by nature, what our background is, what talents we do or do not have, what knowledge we have, what our circumstances are. The thing that determines whether or not we are chosen is how we respond to the calling when we sense God's invitation in our heart, and what fruit we bear as a result. The story of Esther is a great example of being chosen. One great verse includes the words, "chosen for such a time as this". I think we like Esther are chosen for such a time as this. To bring deliverance to the loss and downtrodden and the sinner. You can rejoice in knowing you are chosen. Hallelujah!!

Don't stop praying. Even the best human efforts at communication sometimes let us down. Phone connections break. Computers crash. We sometimes do not understand what people say or mean. But Scripture makes clear that God never fails to hear His faithful people. In 1 Kings 18, Elijah demonstrated the striking contrast between the pagan god Baal and Jehovah God. In a showdown to demonstrate who the true God was, after Baal's prophets had prayed for hours, Elijah taunted them: "Shout louder! . . . Surely, he is a god! Perhaps he is deep in thought, or busy, or traveling. Maybe he is sleeping and must be awakened" (v. 27). Then Elijah prayed for Jehovah to answer so that His chosen people might return to faith, and God's power was clearly displayed. While our prayers may not always be answered as immediately as Elijah's was, we can be assured that God hears them (Psalm 34:17). The Bible reminds us that He treasures our prayers so much that He keeps them before Him in "golden bowls," like precious incense (Revelation 5:8). God will answer every prayer in His own perfect wisdom and way. Thank God that you are chosen for this season and that He always hears you.

CHAPTER 10

Praise! Use Your Weapon

When life gets you down, remember that it's only shaping you to be a stronger version of yourself. When I am struggling, I found that my praise can be a powerful weapon. As you praise the Lord, things begin to happen in the unseen realm. In order to move from purpose to destiny and to live our best life, we must enter into warfare. The enemy will not just stand still and allow you to receive the promises of God. He will fight you at every point along the way.

The weapons of our warfare are not carnal, but mighty through the pulling down of strong holds. In addition to reading the Word of God, Fasting and Praying, and Trusting God, I believe we have an even greater weapon. It is our weapon of praise. You will find throughout the bible, that we are directed to praise. In essence, to praise is to express adoration. We praise the Lord for Who He is, His works, and His character. Praise includes the acts of blessing, commending, honoring, thanking, celebrating, and rejoicing. We praise the Lord because He is worthy of all our praise. Psalm 119:7 (KJV) says: "I will praise you with an upright heart, when I learn your righteous rules." Praise is not motivated by a hypocritical desire to look more "spiritual "; instead, true praise is motivated by seeing and experiencing God's goodness to us and others and by learning the ways of the Lord. In Frank Hammond's book, entitled Praise, A weapon of Warfare and Deliverance, he writes

> As you praise the Lord, things begin to happen in the unseen realm. In the Old Testament, the people of God didn't have the name of Jesus as a weapon, but they did have praise. When Saul was troubled by an evil spirit, the only thing they knew to help him was to call David. What happened when David began to play on his harp and sing praise to his God? The evil spirit departed from King Saul. You can see why praise was so important to those Old Testament saints. You can see why they developed such a lifestyle of praise. We are told to resist the devil and make him flee, and praise is an often overlooked and underused weapon to accomplish this. I want you to understand what your praise does in the spirit realm. A demon cannot exist in that atmosphere — he simply cannot function. Evil spirits have tormented us enough; through praise we get to turn the tables and torment them!

So, when the enemy comes upon you like a flood, The Lord will raise up a standard. Let that standard be your praise. Oftentimes we must remind ourselves to give God the praise no matter what we may be going through. We have to remind ourselves of the faithfulness of God in the moments when it feels darkest. When we offer the sacrifice of praise to God out of obedience, soon enough, we will start to believe it again as well. We do not deny our pain; rather, by praising the Lord, we are choosing to remember that He is there with us in the midst of it. Hoping in God and praising God go together: "But I will hope continually and will praise you yet more and more" (Psalm 71:14). We have the assurance of God's faithfulness. What God has done before He can do again. "Let us hold fast the confession of our hope without wavering, for he who promised is faithful" (Hebrews 10:23 KJV). Psalm 42 shows us the back-and-forth struggle of the sacrifice of praise. The psalmist is in great agony because of his troubles and sorrows; He feels forsaken by God. Instead of turning away, he chooses to remember God's goodness to him in the past. 1 Thessalonians 5:16-18 (KJV) Rejoice always, pray continually, give thanks in all circumstances; for this is God's will for you in Christ Jesus. As we praise God, we will discover incredible benefits for our lives. That's because we were created by God to praise Him. Whatever you do, don't stop praising God, no matter the situation or the circumstance. God is with you when you praise Him, for He inhabits (dwells in) your praise. Your best life begins now. So, let's just praise the Lord.

BIBLIOGRAPHY

Hammond, Frank. Praise, *A Weapon of Warfare and Deliverance*. Impact Christian Books Inc. Kirkwood, MO. 2015.

Strong, James. *Strong Exhaustive Concordance of the Bible*. Hendrickson Publishers Marketing, LLC. Peabody MA. 2007.

The Essential Evangelical Parallel Bible. Updated Edition: New King James Version, English Standard Version, New Living Translation, The Message. Oxford University Press, Inc. New York, NY. 2004.

The Merriam-Webster Dictionary. https://www.merriam-webster.com retrieved October 21, 2020.